Introduction

No STYLE HAS BEEN AS LONG LASTING OR
AS UNIVERSALLY ENJOYED AS COUNTRY.
Although the term style suggests a planned
design that is at odds with the basic unself-
consciousness of country homes, it is used
here because certain rural traditions have
deeply influenced international styles of furniture, and it is these that have been featured
in this book.

It can be argued that country style cannot
be transplanted since it relies on the very
landscapes and nuances of light from
whence it grew. Yet scores of photographs
throughout these pages illustrate just how
successfully elements of these styles have
been exported worldwide. The distinctive
features of *le style Provençal* – the golden
patinated furniture and printed fabrics – can
be purchased all over the world. So, too, can
Swedish painted furniture and tables, chairs

and boxes inspired by the Shaker tradition.
With a little research, these objects can be
happily adapted to fit within a city apartment or a country cottage.

To an extent it is still true that country
style, which belonged essentially to the
poor, can be achieved without spending a
lot of money. It comes from a tradition of
simplicity and making do. But while this
book celebrates authentic country furniture
it is not a call to deprivation or hardship.

Most of us have a picture in our mind of
what country living is all about. It may be
the comfortable clutter of the English cottage, or it may include the aroma of drying
herbs and baking bread. The magic of country style lies in its naturalness, honesty of
design and directness. In this sense, creating
a country style requires the opposite of
effort; it succeeds most where it tries least.

Above: *Because fine woods were scarce in colonial America, most furniture was made from inferior wood and then painted.* **Opposite:** *A Windsor chair in the corner of a dining room with soft green panelling.*

CONTENTS

The Country
Furniture Companion

The Country
Furniture Companion

Judith and Martin Miller

Photography by James Merrell

MITCHELL BEAZLEY

The Country Furniture Companion
Judith and Martin Miller

First published in Great Britain 1995
by Mitchell Beazley
an imprint of Reed Consumer Books Limited
Michelin House, 81 Fulham Road, London SW3 6RB
and Auckland, Melbourne, Singapore and Toronto

Photography by *James Merrell*
Illustrations by *James Croft*

Art Editor	*Peta Waddington*
Editors	*Sophie Pearse and Jonathan Hilton*
Art Director	*Jacqui Small*
Executive Editor	*Judith More*
Production	*Heather O'Connell*

A CIP record for this book is available from the British Library

ISBN 1 85732 448 X

The publishers have made every effort to ensure that all instructions given in this book are accurate and safe, but they cannot accept liability for any resulting injury, damage or loss to either person or property, whether direct or consequential and howsoever arising. The authors and publishers will be grateful for any information which will assist them in keeping future editions up to date.

Colour reproduction by Rival Colour, UK
Produced by Mandarin Offset
Printed and bound in China

TRADITIONAL COUNTRY

Opposite: *A traditional Orkney chair in a house designed in the Scottish vernacular.*
Above: *Seating provided by a Baptist church pew and Chippendale-style chairs.*

COUNTRY STYLE RUNS THROUGH THE HISTORY OF INTERIOR DECORATION LIKE SOME SORT OF DURABLE THREAD. Simple, instinctive and traditional, it was created by those without the money to follow new trends. It is not hard to understand why it has outlasted the changling fashions of the rich.

If there is a current vogue for traditional country it is not a new one. The simplicity at the heart of the country look answers an old impulse in those who have the money and possessions to experiment with having less. "Country" became established as a sought-after style in the 19th century, when, as a reaction to the bourgeois excesses of the period, the rural interior became the symbol not just of an ideal way of life but of a fast-disappearing one.

Traditional county style today remains based on the fundamentals of simplicity and a love of craftsmanship. Since it belonged to the poor, and was born of the necessity to make do, the style can still be achieved without spending much money.

The magic of traditional country is that it is created from elements that are almost too wholesome – naturalness, honesty of design, directness – yet it has more warmth and appeal than any other style.

ENGLISH

If traditional country style is the answer to the universal daydream of the simple life, then the English cottage is its precise location. Inside its weathered, honey-colored Cotswold-stone walls there is an immediate impression of clutter; it is as if the occupants once lived somewhere much larger.

The pine kitchen dresser, overflowing with elegant blue-and-white china – used only for special occasions – is crammed up against side tables that are heaped with books, and oak chairs and tables crowd near oversized fireplaces while seats fit snugly under the windows in the deep recesses afforded by thick walls.

Moving up the social scale, larger country homes enjoyed a more spacious interior and often incorporated finer pieces of furniture of the period. Often, however, this furniture would have been freely interpreted by provincial craftsmen in order to provide generally more practical, less-delicate pieces, such as oak buffets and country-style ladderback chairs. The 19th-century Arts and Crafts architect Charles Voysey urged people toward plainness, with interiors consisting of "simple oak furniture and nothing in it but necessary articles of use."

Opposite: *A 19th-century Cornish Windsor chair in front of a cast-iron fireplace.* **Above:** *Practical furniture and hard-wearing surfaces are hallmarks of English country style.* **Below:** *A variety of 19th-century chairs surround a mellow pine table.*

NORTH EUROPEAN

The country style most readily associated with northern Europe is that of Scandinavia, especially that of the provincial Swedish farmhouse. These rural northern communities are among the most isolated in Europe, and there is much in the interior of the traditional Scandinavian farmhouse that is familiar from the pioneer homes of early America.

Opposite: *The inset panels, carved details and turned legs on these Swedish chairs indicate an innate sense of style, yet one perfectly adapted to country life.* **Above left:** *A closet fits snugly between 18th-century built-in beds.* **Above right:** *Two tiers of built-in beds and, in front, stools that double as ingenious storage boxes.*

Scandinavia has close historic associations with France, and in 1818 Napoleon's marshal, Jean-Baptiste-Jules Bernadotte, became ruler of Sweden. The French influence created rural interiors that combine decoration and simplicity, so while traditional stools remained by the fireside, grander pieces were arranged around the walls. Fixed benches gave way to delicate chairs, often locally made but based on shapes popular in France. The original, simpler furniture was not supplanted, mainly because it was often built-in. Traditional chairs had folding backs or wide seats to convert them into fireside tables for meals. Some had boxes beneath for storage. Beds were built into the walls and cabinets and stoves fitted into corners.

SOUTH EUROPEAN

The climate leaves an indelible impression on both the architecture and the furniture of any region.

The look that is labelled as French country has been deeply influenced by the style of the southern region of Provence, bordered on one side by the Rhône and the other by the Mediterranean. The colors of the landscape are repeated indoors to draw in the view from behind the flaking shutters.

In the furnishings and on painted furniture, colors are grouped as they are outside – in eye-catching contrasts of jangling intensity. The Provençal style owes much to the Mediterranean ports, and craftsmen from all over France were attracted to the region during the 18th and 19th centuries. Boxes, chairs and cabinets ordered by wealthy farmers were often handsomely carved. Poorer smallholders could probably pay for just one embellished piece, which was likely to be a general-purpose cabinet for food and clothes – the *armoire* – which was made of local walnut. The rest of the furniture was built along far more simple lines, including box-frame beds, rush-seated benches, plain dining tables and the bentwood chair.

If Italian country style has but one color, it is terra cotta – the rich red earth color of the landscape of Tuscany. The furniture of this region is simple, but the plainest lines are dramatized when set against the granular walls and battered paint. This contrast lends a sculptural quality to the most ordinary of chairs. Wooden chests and dressers are unpainted, while decorative detail is provided by wrought-iron shaped into bedheads.

The style of southern Spain was shaped by the hot landscape. Spanish country furniture is simple: sofas are no more than daybeds and benches might be built out from the wall in slabs of stone. Chairs are rush-seated in unpainted yew or pine. The modern coffee table is appropriate here, as are rich mahogany woods that contrast so well with the backdrop of brilliant whitewash.

Opposite: *A French 18th-century beech ladderback chair harmonizes with a 19th-century chestnut desk.*
Above: *An 18th-century* armoire, *containing a concealed bed, surrounded by Louis XVI dining chairs.*

AMERICAN

A merican country style is the style of an independent people. Many of its most-loved features are those created by the early pioneers as they set up home up and down the Atlantic coast during the 17th century.

The isolation of these communities produced a variety of distinct regional styles, from that of the Ohio farmhouse set among the mid-West's rolling planes to the Cape Cod cottage perched by the sea. And as the style of house was markedly different from region to region, so, too, was the way that they were furnished and decorated.

Like farmers everywhere, the settlers built and furnished their homes using materials most readily to hand, but with the difference

stenciling was used as a way of decorating chairs and chests. The interiors of Cape Cod cottages conjured up memories of England, and furniture consisted of what they had brought with them and simple pieces made on arrival based on designs from home, such as low-backed Windsor chairs. In the South, English pieces were brought in the holds of trade ships and so rustic versions of Georgian designs gradually appeared in rural homes. By the same route, furniture designed for ships, like the lightweight rattan steamer chair, made its way into southerners' homes.

Opposite: *A restored 18th-century Rhode Island interior.* **Above:** *An 18th-century yellow pine table flanked by 19th-century ladderback chairs.* **Below:** *Yellow birch rockers with woven ash backs and seats.*

that they were often influenced by the traditions of their countries of origin. What American country styles do have in common, however, is wood. At first it was crudely worked, but as the tools and skills developed, America's wood was polished turned, planed and fretted to produce furniture whose decorativeness is often in stark contrast to the rooms in which it is found.

The Dutch and Germans who came to Pennsylvania brought their memories of folk art traditions, and squares of pierced tin were used for the fronts of cabinets, and

SHAKER

L ed by an Englishwoman, Ann Lee, the Shakers were one of a number of Utopian sects that migrated to America during the 18th century. The communal ideals of the Shakers led to a desire for a rigid uniformity of style throughout their many scattered communities. However, everything they made or used was of the highest quality. Work was a form of worship and the appearance of Shaker goods should be as pure and as simple as Shaker prayers.

18

The interiors of Shaker houses were light, plain and simple. Storage was often built-in, and their clever designs for walls of cabinets and smooth-fitting drawers have never been bettered. Tables and benches were plain and always beautifully proportioned. Objects that might clutter the room, such as tools, chairs and clocks were hung high up on walls when not in use. Furniture was typically painted in cheerful colors, and storage boxes were often color-coded. Figured woods were also used for furniture, and chair seats were made of cane, wood splints or fabric tape. The Shaker ladderback chair, which is light-weight and harmonious in its proportions, is eloquent testimony of the sect's sensitivity to good design.

Opposite: *Shaker-style peg rails provide storage space.* **Above:** *Built-in cupboards are authentic to Shaker style.* **Below:** *An uncluttered Shaker bedroom; the rocking chair dates from around 1830.*

CONTEMPORARY RUSTIC

Opposite and Above: *This furniture, by the American designer Gustav Stickley (1857-1942), is made of oak and harks back in some respects to the design style of the Shakers.*

COUNTRY STYLE IS NOT SIMPLY ABOUT LOOKING RETROSPECTIVELY AT PAST STYLES, FASHIONS AND TRADITIONS. Instead, the very essence of country style is its continuing absorption of the world around it, for it is a living, ever-evolving style. Well-made new pieces, which have simple lines and are constructed from natural materials, can be used to furnish converted old country barns, farmhouses or cottages thanks to the involvement of many new and innovative furniture designers. And nor does country style necessitate a cluttered environment – there is plenty of scope for settings that are quite spare and peaceful.

Just as the original homes of rural people evolved as each generation matured – the furniture was added to, exchanged and eventually discarded – so their modern counterparts can also defy period definition. Even though country furniture was primarily utilitarian and often simply made, it was not necessarily without ornamentation. Solid, practical pieces were often painted, for example, in order to cover the deficiencies in the wood as well as for the sheer pleasure of the decoration. This same look can be adapted today to improve modern pieces that look too new and raw for a country setting.

NEW CRAFTSMEN

William Morris, who rebelled against the mass production brought about by the Industrial Revolution, insisted on truth to materials and honesty of design, and thus laid the foundations of the Arts and Crafts Movement at the close of the 19th century. The Movement found enthusiastic support in parts of America, where it became known as the "Craftsman style".

The emphasis was on craftsmanship, high-quality of materials and the use of the right material for a specific purpose. Although inspired by the workmanship, and sometimes the motifs, of the Middle Ages, these designer-craftsmen were not aping former styles. The furniture they produced was certainly true to a long tradition, but the style they created was new and totally original.

Their furniture was usually plain and upright and often constructed of oak decorated with simple cut-out motifs, such as hearts or spearheads – an approach in keeping with the long tradition of country furniture making.

One of the most important and influential 20th-century designers of the late Arts and Crafts style in the Eastern states of America was Gustav Stickley. As well as being a furniture maker, Stickley was also the editor of the

Opposite: *A modern elm coffer, one of a set of six cut in the round.* **Above:** *Modern furniture perfectly at home in a medieval priory.* **Below:** *The shape of the table echoes the strong lines of the beams.*

Craftsman Magazine for the first 16 years of the 20th century. He was well known for his great belief in "simplicity of construction" and most of his pieces are stamped with the Stickley motto – *Als Ik Kan*, which literally translates as "All I Can". These three simple words perfectly embody the character, spirit and attitude of the Movement.

The furniture of contemporary designer and craftsman Richard Latrobe Bateman, whose work is illustrated on these pages, is again part of this same tradition. His work is entirely modern, yet it still retains an unbreakable bond with the traditions of the past, in terms of its strength and purity of conception and execution. And the naturalness and honesty of design of work such as this makes it extremely adaptable in terms of its setting and the styles of the other furniture and ornamentation against which it is seen.

SALVAGE

In a world where natural resources have been plundered by generations of people who have assumed that nature's bounty was without end, there is now a growing awareness that this folly must end.

Each and every year, an area of the world's forest approximately the size of England is destroyed forever. In just about 45 years – since 1950 – tropical rainforests have shrunk from an area covering about 30 percent of the world's land surface to the mere 7-10 percent that remains today. Much of this devastation is the result of the seemingly insatiable demand for hardwoods, such as

Above: *Salvaged timber combined with driftwood produce an authentically ethnic coffee table.*

teak and mahogany, in which the rainforests are particularly rich, for use by the building and furniture industries. Once cleared of its tree cover, the topsoil is soon lost to erosion by wind and rain and so the forests can no longer regenerate.

One way of lessening the load on our diminishing natural resources is to refashion, revamp and reuse as much as possible. The country tradition has always been one of thrift and economy, born of a constant struggle to wrest a living from an often hard and unforgiving environment. Nothing that could be salvaged would ever be wasted. Scraps of cloth would be carefully collected

Above: *A restful effect is created by teaming salvaged wood with subdued and natural colors.*

and saved and eventually turned into patchwork quilts; old sacking material would be transformed into work clothes or hung to cover bare walls; pieces of old tin were cut and elaborately shaped to decorate the fronts of cabinets; nails were restraightened and used time and time again; and wood that was salvaged from barns, obsolete and abandoned buildings or unwanted pieces of furniture was reworked to suit the requirements of the latest generation.

The scope today for reusing salvaged wood is immense, particularly because so much furniture is simply discarded as fashions change from season to season or it is

Above: *A seasoned plank bench, a fruit box wall display and a seed tray used as shelving.*

Above: *The rough-hewn appearance of this salvaged timber was enhanced by grit-blasting.*

often scrapped when buildings are refurbished. Once stripped of its painted or varnished finish, or planed back in order to remove the worst of gouges, scrapes and nail holes, it can be brought back into use in its original form or dissembled and rebuilt as new pieces of furniture. As well as the economy, old wood has a character and an integrity – the patina of age – that only comes after years of use.

Another source of salvaged wood comes from the sea. Driftwood can be beautiful in itself, sculptural and elegant; but it can also be accessorized with natural textures such as cotton, wicker and coir.

CLASSIC MODERN COUNTRY

It is becoming increasingly difficult to distinguish between country style and sheer nostalgia, where almost anything goes as long as it is old - or at least has the appearance of being old. But the new should not be ruled out, as the homes shown on these pages prove.

Country style is liberating because, having evolved continuously over a period of many centuries, it cannot be forced into any one time peiod, or era. The keys to an understanding of this style, be it authentically old or an example of classic modern country, is the combination of the naturalness of the materials used and an honesty and simplicity in the design.

There really is no good reason to hunt out old or antique pieces merely because you live in a country-style home, unless of course that is your preference, or you enjoy the hunt. Neither is it necessary to live in a country-style cottage or farmhouse in order to furnish it with traditional pieces.

When set against the sloping roof and the wall timbers of a traditional old building, a modern-built four-poster bed will sit quite comfortably alongside contemporary wicker chairs, replacement plain wood rooflight

Above: *Supporting beams have been utilized to hold the white drapes of a modern four-poster.*
Below: *Rough-plastered walls, stone and wood add ethnic texture to this modern French room.*

Above: *Siena was the inspirational starting point for this Tuscan-style home set in London, England.*
Below: *Touches of color – blue, orange and cream – echo the traditional hues of Provence.*

frames and safety balustrades. And when handled with care, sensitivity and a sureness of touch, modern upholstered furniture can be very successfully integrated into country-style rooms dominated by an open fireplace and the rustic textures of rough plaster walls, stone and wood.

To indulge yourself a little and introduce an element of fantasy into your home, why not use the classic modern country style of one country to conjure up an environment that is totally different to the one in which you live? However, here some care needs to be exercised, for if the effect is to be seamless then the furniture, accessories, ornamentation, paint colors and even the lighting, must all come together to transform the setting into a believable facsimilie. A half-hearted attempt could result in your room looking more like a stage set.

Since "country" is a living, organic style, it is immensely adaptable and open to endless interpretation. But, like the strands of a web stretching from the past into the present, the inherent principles of simplicity, functionality and integrity that underlie country style, link the different eras together, thus allowing the genuinely old and rustic to be used alongside the classic modern.

PAINTED FURNITURE

28

Opposite and above: *The well-worn painted furniture and decorative motifs give an impression of informal and relaxed comfort.*

THE MODERN TREND OF STRIPPING WOOD OF ITS ORIGINAL PAINT FINISH HAS, SADLY, DONE MUCH TO DESTROY AN IMPORTANT ASPECT OF THE HISTORY OF TRADITIONAL FURNITURE. Although often primitive in its construction, county-style furniture did not eschew decoration or ornamentation. Our forebears discovered that one of the easiest ways of adding a touch of brightness to the often somewhat austere interiors of their cottages or farmhouses was to apply coats of home-made paint – which could be easily made from ingredients that were readily to hand – to tables, cabinets, dressers, chairs, bedheads and so on.

As fashions changed, so did colors. By carefully removing the layers of paintwork built up over the centuries, you will soon discover what hue was fashionable in different periods. If you have restoration in mind, then look at examples of period pieces that have escaped the heat gun and chemical stripper – many of the colors are not difficult to emulate.

Apply different-colored coats patchily onto the bare wood, then paint on an even top coat. Rub the paint with damp wet-and-dry paper to reveal the underlying color and grain. Years of use can be simulated by rubbing back the areas of most wear.

PAINT TYPES

The most frequently used hand-mixed paints, for well over of 600 years, were simple whitewashes and colorwashes. To make these, natural pigments were added to the whitewash to give hues in the ranges of ocher yellow or red, blues and greens. In addition, limewashes were also frequently applied. These had slaked lime – water added to calcium oxide – as their main constituent, and they seem to have been popular because of their disinfectant qualities.

A more glossy finish was achieved by using paints that had a proportion of oils, waxes, or even milk mixed into the paint base. These were the forerunners of today's paints. The glossy finish was predominantly used on indoor woodwork from about the middle of the 17th century. We now know that all but the finest-quality wood was painted – our present preference for stripped pine doors and furniture would have seemed very odd indeed to our ancestors.

Toward the end of the 18th century, some townhouses had another treatment applied in which water-based painted backgrounds were "distressed" or "scumbled" with oil paints in order to produce the decorative effect of marbling or graining.

Opposite: *Scarred paint on a time-worn dresser.*
Above: *This English mahogany settle was stripped and then painted with a white wood stain.*
Below: *A whitewashed 18th-century Welsh press.*

COLORS

Choice of paint color and painted design varies from country to country, as well between regions within the same country, with each particular place tending to have its own traditions. The Provençal look, for example, is one of the most decorative of all the varied "country" styles, and starkly plain, whitewashed walls are likely to be interrupted by a sky-blue internal door or a citrus-yellow cabinet.

In Tuscany, by way of a contrast, furniture made from locally grown, good-quality chestnut was most often left unpainted, while inferior woods would be heavily disguised by being decorated with painted flowers or landscape scenes executed in a thin, flat watercolor to emulate the ornate layers of the richer man's furniture.

In America, the abundance of wood gave the country-style interior a surface for paint-work that gleamed softly in deep, full colors, such as bottle-green, teal and reddish-brick.

The colors were used in counterpoint to each other – the matchboarding on the walls perhaps painted blue-green, the door a deep brick and a small cabinet a vivid turquoise. This geometry of colors is a hallmark of American rural interiors, inspired by the inexpensiveness of paints, which were made in the home from milk and natural pigments.

The *chiaroscuro* of light and dark is the hall-mark of Spanish country style. Just as tickets to a bullfight are sold as *sol* (sun) or *sombra* (shade), so the Spanish interiors do not compromise with the sun. Instead of the sun-warmed tones of Italy, the colors of Spanish style tend to be fiery or very cool. White is a constant foil to the dark furniture, richly colored rugs and brightly glazed tiles. The contrasts are multiplied when solid walls are punctuated with open-work patterns, shutters pierced with filigree and hard floors softened with kelims.

Opposite: *A Mexican cabinet and a Jamaican stool.* **Above left:** *Painted furniture teamed with bright colors on the floor and walls.* **Above right:** *Paint color used to create a theme.* **Below left:** *A Canadian example of the time-worn charm of painted furniture.* **Below right:** *A streaked and grained clothes press.*

PATTERNS

Just as flat areas of single-colored paint were often applied to enliven the inside of rural dwellings – or, just as frequently, to disguise the use of poor-quality wood – so, too, were more ambitious examples of painted patterns and motifs a common feature of much country-style furniture. In Scandinavia, the Swedish King Gustav III sent out artists from Stockholm during the 17th century to plunder the rococo and neo-classical styles of France. Slowly, these borrowings from France made their way from the homes of the nobility into the houses of the farmers. This ornate decorative style was spread, in measured steps, by traveling artists who might paint a family's closet or wardrobe, for example, or their bedhead and frame.

The Provençal exhibitionism of pattern and color has made its prints famous throughout the world. The bright fabrics were originally based on the East India Company's cottons, which

Opposite: *Exaltations of nature are a common decorative theme on Alpine furniture.* **Above left:** *This carved and painted 19th-century Scandinavian bed has a cupboard built in at the foot.* **Above right:** *A very fine example of a Swedish cupboard, dating from 1774, decorated with painted flowers.*

arrived in bundles on the Marseille quayside, but their splendid decorative tradition extends to the furniture as well. Whereas a rich land owner might commission pieces of fine furniture decorated with handsomely carved sheaves of corn and knots of myrtle leaves or scrolls of music to symbolize a cultured household, a poorer farmer might settle for something more within his means. Instead of carved furniture, typical furniture decoration might consist of a painted theme of ribbons of fruit and flowers on chest fronts and chair tops.

CLASSIC PIECES

Opposite: *Although French in design and construction, this armoire is in a London kitchen.*
Above: *This Shaker rocker has the timeless elegance of all well-made country pieces.*

BECAUSE OF BOTH THE SHEER ELEGANCE OF THEIR CONCEPTION AND THE FUNCTIONALITY OF THEIR DESIGN SOME PIECES OF FURNITURE HAVE DEVELOPED A TRULY ENDURING AND TIMELESS APPEAL.

Such an example is the classic French *armoire*, (see opposite) which can be found fashioned in a variety of inexpensive softwoods and more costly hardwoods. The durability of a piece of furniture such as this is amply testified to when you consider that, originally, it would have been intended for the storing of weapons.

These classic pieces of design are now highly sought-after and often pressed into service as elegant storage receptacles for linen or clothes – or, if located in a kitchen environment, then as cabinets for displaying prized pieces of glassware, pottery or china. And you are as likely to find one in an innercity Parisian apartment as a Provençal farmhouse.

Another example of the magic certain pieces of design can exert is the rocking chair, which, although only a relative newcomer, has become so firmly entrenched in people's minds that it is now synonymous with country style. It must, therefore, be counted as one of the "classic" pieces.

Above: *Simply elegant, a pine table and chairs positioned to receive maximum light from the small window.*
Opposite: *A 19th-century pine sideboard in the wood-lined parlor of a comfortable English farmhouse.*

PINE

Due to its distribution throughout the world, furniture made from pine is a common feature of country style in many countries. Not only is it commonly used for furniture, pine has also been used to build houses, barns and outbuildings in countries as far apart as Russia, Switzerland, Britain, Japan and the length and breadth of North America. The traditional frontier log cabin, home of the early American pioneers, would have been constructed from massive pine logs – a building style that was brought to the New World along with the settlers from the colder regions of Europe.

Today we are most familiar with country pine furniture in its stripped form. Because pine grows so widely and quickly, it was commonly used to furnish the homes of poorer farmers and land workers. Not only would pine be the main component used to make furniture such as tables, beds, chairs, dressers and cabinets, it would also line the walls, cover the bare earth of the floors and even fuel the fires. It should not be thought, however, that all pieces of pine furniture were crudely made, nor were the design, care and detailing employed necessarily inferior to pieces made of the rich man's

oak, teak, and mahogany. Indeed, many examples of rustic pine furniture hundreds of years old survive today and are considered to be classic pieces of design and craftsmanship. In order to disguise the deficiencies inherent in the wood, many of these pieces would originally have been painted, either in a flat overall color or decorated with motifs based on the natural world, such as flowers, animals or leaf designs. Either because the paint has not withstood the passage of the years or because of changing fashions, it is now uncommon to find old pine that has not been stripped back to its raw state.

OAK

Forests of mighty oak trees once proliferated throughout the temperate regions of Europe and North America. For hundreds, even thousands, of years our ancestors felled these hardwood forest giants to provide their necessary shelter, to build furniture from, to carve and decorate, and to revere. And, of course, it was the oak that provided the principal lumber from which the great colonizing European navies were constructed. But the price was high – the construction of a single, large 18th-century warship required lumber equivalent to more than 4,000 fully grown trees, and this meant the destruction of some 80 acres of mature oak forest. Today, thankfully, a large percentage of the oak supplied to the building and furniture industries derives from managed plantations.

Oak is most certainly the right choice of wood for the look of the Medieval style, which tends toward simplicity and sparseness. Plainly constructed chests, benches, box-style armchairs, settees and, especially, trestle tables, as well as built-in cupboards and seats in the

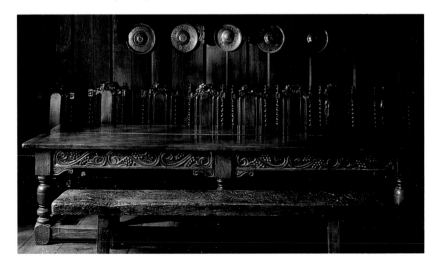

Opposite: *A wonderful 17th-century carved refectory table with a simple bench and a set of 17th-century chairs ranked behind.* **Above left:** *A fine 16th-century carved oak chair creates a medieval atmosphere.* **Above right:** *An early 18th-century country style oak chair framed by a simply painted stairway.*

same style, are the correct pieces to choose for recreating the furnishings of this period. And the wood should preferably not be blackened – this was a 19th-century fashion. Oak furniture of this style can be left plain or matte-painted in brick-red or dark green, perhaps with detailing picked out in gold. By the 16th and 17th centuries, furniture was much more in evidence than was the case previously. Oak was still the first choice for those who could afford it and the practice of painting and gilding furniture still continued; oak might be painted red, blue, green or black. It is hard to know what the original color of unpainted oak furniture would have been. While it was certainly waxed or oiled, and sometimes limed to darken it to a mid-brown color – unlike the pale limed oak of the 1920s – we can be fairly certain that it was not stained black, as was popular in the late 19th century. Some pieces – especially tables, beds and cupboards built to impress guests – were large and heavy, with rich carving in an amalgamation of Renaissance and Gothic motifs or with strapwork decoration.

FRUITWOOD

Although we normally think of fruit trees in terms of the edible crops they produce, their lumber, too, figures strongly in country-style furniture. The country ethos abhors waste

Opposite: *An attractive 18th-century fruitwood wine table stands beside a fireplace.* **Above left:** *Late 18th-century rush-seated ladderback chairs alongside a Windsor settee are grouped around a settle table.* **Above right:** *Shafts of sunlight highlight an 18th-century Provençal fruitwood buffet.*

of any description, and once a tree had come to the end of its productive life in the orchard it would be uprooted to be reborn as tables, chairs, cabinets and even as precision parts for machinery. The hard, close-grained characteristics of apple wood, for example, made it an ideal material from which to make the toothed gear wheels of wind mills, and American long-case clocks sometimes featured gear wheels made of apple or cherry wood. In Mediterranean regions olive wood figures strongly in country style, especially for small, carved, decorative items, bowls and ornaments. The straight-grained wood of the cherry, with its attractive pale pinkish-brown color, lends itself easily to furniture making and cabinetwork, while pear wood is to be found as fine inlay and marquetry.

WALNUT

The term walnut is often used to refer to a number of brown-colored woods with attractive, pronounced grains. The true walnut, however, comes from the species *Juglans*, which is found growing in the warmer regions of the northern hemisphere and right through central and southern America. In Canada and the United States the darker *Juglans nigra*, is to be found.

The demand for different woods at different times in history has been a matter of fashion, but the decorative qualities of walnut has meant that it has always been reserved for the finer examples of country-style furniture. During the English Baroque period, which coincided with the restoration to the English throne of the flamboyant Charles II in 1660, walnut began to oust oak as the fashionable wood for furniture making, and better pieces were often inlaid with marquetry. The same basic shapes and styles of furniture also came into fashion in North America, and some pieces were imported from England and then copied by local craftsmen. Some of the distinguishing features of this furniture of this era are narrow, high backs to chairs with scrolled or barley-twist legs and carved tops. Moving on to the beginning of the 18th century, walnut pieces of furniture with cabriole legs were more characteristic of the time – dining chairs, wing-chairs and sofas, writing tables, dressing tables, chests of drawers, dome-topped bureaus and bookcases. In England, this fashion for furniture made of walnut lasted until about 1720, when mahogany began to be imported. The fashion for mahogany lasted right through to the late 19th century, when there was a resurgence of interest in walnut furniture.

Opposite: *An attractive early 19th-century walnut bureau and a modern ladderback chair give a period feel to this comfortable writing area.* **Above:** *The solid form of a French-made 18th-century walnut buffet laden with antique pewterware stands out starkly against a simple cream-colored wall.*

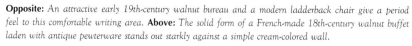

LADDERBACK CHAIRS

The ladderback chair, so called because of its distinctive arrangement of cross-pieces, like the rungs of a ladder, forming the chair back, is truly a keynote of international country style. The detail of the ladderback varies from country to country, but the basic design

Opposite: *A painted and stenciled ladderback makes an attractive kitchen addition.* **Above left:** *Contemporary Shaker-style ladderbacks.* **Above right:** *An 18th-century North American ladderback.*

remains the same. In English country tradition, the ladderback is most closely associated with the 18th century. The solid, robust versions of the chair design, appropriate to rural life, can be found in simple pine and better quality fruitwood, oak and walnut. Across the Atlantic, in North America ladderback chairs can be found in Amish communities and, in a slightly different form, the ladderback is also closely associated with the Shakers. Often with seats woven from rush, which could be harvested near to hand, or with colorful fabric tapes, the ladderback was the Shaker solution to the need for seating that was sturdy yet light enough to be hung up out of the way on wooden pegs fixed onto battens that ran around the room.

ROCKING CHAIRS

As with other types of furniture, chair designs evolved to suit local require-ments and were, by necessity, governed by the practicalities of rural life and the avail-ability of local materials. In colder climates, chairs that enveloped the occupant made good, practical sense in order to keep drafts away and so provide extra comfort, and you can see how wing chairs would have been particularly valued in this regard.

In a very different climate, in the deep South of America, a type of chair design

Below: *The decorative qualities of bark have been used to good effect in this rocker.* **Above:** *American Adirondack furniture incorporates organic forms, such as twigs, branches and roots, into its design.*

evolved that proved admirably suitable for those long, still afternoons and evenings, when the only sensible reaction to the often oppressive heat was to drift lazily off to sleep. The rocking chair is this masterpiece of country design.

Although there is no record of the rocking chair before the 19th century, since that time it has become firmly and seamlessly entrenched as an integral part of country style throughout the United States, Canada and many other countries of the world. Those same Atlantic trading ships that brought with them the latest furniture styles and fancies from England during the 19th century would also have taken back in their holds examples of "colonial" workmanship, innovation and adaptation to local conditions. Now, of course, many people would be truly surprised not to see, for example, a rocking chair as part of the cottage clutter that so typifies English country style.

Many different communities adopted the rocking chair as part of their own furniture tradition, and each, inevitably, brought to it their own way of life and philosophies.

Above: *A modern Amish rocking chair is ideal to furnish an American country porch or verandah.*
Below: *Rocking chairs, such as this 19th-century example, were a North American innovation.*

In Indiana, for example, the abundant hickory tree was pressed into service, and the wood for rockers was first boiled to make it pliable and then bent over metal frames and thin pieces were soaked and then woven for seating. While in a typical Shaker design you can see the simplicity and elegance of their conception, and the skill of their craftsmanship is undeniable. And the more elaborate Adirondack variation shows the organic fluidity associated with the rustic ideal underlying this 19th-century back-to-nature movement.

STOOLS

The major consideration in the design and construction of rural furniture was practicality. The more simply and therefore inexpensively a piece of furniture could be made, the

more successful it was likely to be. In this regard, in early country houses, especially those

Opposite: *Pivoting legs make this design easy to store when not in use.* **Above left:** *Stools with chair backs provide extra comfort.* **Above right:** *A carved chief's stool from the northwest coast of America.*

belonging to poorer people, stools and benches were to be more commonly found than chairs, which required more materials and a high degree of skill to make. What chairs did exist would often be reserved for special guests and visitors or for the head of the household. Both three- and four-leg stool designs are to be found, with the tripod arrangement proving remarkably stable on the type of uneven flooring surface typically found in country homes.

Other cultures and far older civilizations also developed the stool as part of their tradition. In some African tribes, for example, there are to be found different ranks of stools, with varying degrees of elaboration and ornamentation depending on the social status of the owner. The tombs of ancient Egypt, too, have revealed that the god-like ruling pharaohs would count the stool among their worldly possessions worthy enough to take with them to the afterlife.

CHESTS

The different types, styles, functions and methods of construction of chests are extremely diverse. One of the earliest chests known to have existed was a very crude affair with a small cavity hewn in the middle of a large section of wooden tree trunk. A hinged lid finished off the design and the sheer bulk of the construction would have made the contents secure indeed. Round-lidded chests became common during the 14th century. These slab-sided boxes were built up from substantial pieces of wooden planks, reinforced with spikes and secured with iron bands fixed in place by the local

blacksmith. A common type of country furniture that derived from the round-lidded chest, which looked very like a traditional sea chest, was the flat-topped blanket box. As its name implies, this type of chest would have been used for storing spare bedding, linen or other items of value in the home. And once the lid was down, the chest would then convert to make a convenient table top for meals or a seat to draw up to the hearth.

Whereas some chests had a top that lifted up to reveal the main storage space as well as one or two pull-out drawers beneath, other chests evolved into the chests of drawers that we are all familiar with today. The chest of drawers made its appearance in the middle of the 17th century. The material from which the piece was made reflected the financial standing of the owner. Crudely made pine chests could always be painted in bright colors to hide the poor materials and craftsmanship, while oak, mahogany, elm or ash chests of drawers, if well made, would be left plain, and simply oiled or waxed to provide protection for the wood.

Today, country-style chests can be found in any room, providing invaluable and attractive storage solutions in kitchens, bedrooms, bathrooms and dining rooms.

Opposite: *Two sea chests provide storage space.* **Above:** *This chest is an example of tramp art – a form of applied folk decoration.* **Below:** *A 19th-century painted chest-of-drawers, Italian in origin.*

CUPBOARDS

Obviously, it is neither desirable nor practical to imitate the living standards of a country-style medieval, 18th-century or even a 19th-century household. Clearly, we demand high standards of comfort, lighting, heating and so on that were never dreamed possible in the past. However, along with these standards of comfort and efficiency come the associated problems of modern-day clutter.

One solution to the problem of clutter is, as it has always been in the past, the ever-useful and ubiquitous cupboard – freestanding or wall-mounted – and decorated to blend in with its surroundings or, if its quality is sufficiently good, featured to make a statement.

In the country home, cupboards of one type or another can be pressed into service in virtually every room. In the bedroom, cupboards are to be found crammed with hanging clothes, shoes beneath on the floor space and hats above on a convenient shelf and belts, ties and other items needed for day-to-day living can hang from hooks. In the bathroom, cupboards are likely to contain articles of toiletry – soaps and scents, washcloths, cleansing products – as well as medicines and first-aid paraphernalia. If you are fortunate, you may still be able to obtain marble-topped cupboards with a bowl inset for washing and space to the side for a jug of water to stand.

But it is in the kitchen that the cupboard really comes into its own. Pots, pans, cutlery, linen, preserved and canned food, all can be arranged inside on built-in shelving and conveniently shut away from view when not in use, or displayed to best advantage simply by opening the doors. It is the perfect storage solution, and styles – whether natural finish or painted, plain or carved – can be found or adapted to suit any period of country home.

Opposite: *A cool Mediterranean setting for a fine 18th-century Andalucian food cupboard.* **Above:** *This North American pie safe has holes punched in the tin-fronted panels to allow air to circulate freely inside.*

Above: *A painted interior highlights the colorful china.* **Opposite right:** *A set of shelves added to a cupboard makes an informal dresser.* **Opposite far right:** *A Pennsylvania "Dutch" dresser and chairs.*

DRESSERS

Ask anyone what piece of furniture they most immediately associate with country style and, in nearly every case, the answer will be: the kitchen dresser. In country and provincial districts, styles in furniture and decoration were more informal than in the cities. And at a time when communications were at best rudimentary there was also an inevitable time lag

before the latest city fashions reached out into the rural hinterland. So it was not until the final years of the 18th century that the dresser – this most successful and useful piece of furniture ever devised – began to make its appearance in country regions. Prized for its stylish look, it is able to bring a feel of the country to the most urban of kitchens. The success of the dresser is primarily due to the fact that it is so very practical. The wide, flat shelf above the cupboard makes an ideal extra food preparation surface, while beneath there is a copious storage area for all of the scores of items that won't fit comfortably into the drawers. The shelved display area is designed for your best crockery and the whole unit is wide and tall rather than deep – making it suitable even for smaller kitchens.

in the settler pioneer homes of 17th-century North America, especially when rooms had to serve several purposes. Fold-up tables and those with detachable tops were popular for the same reason, since these could be put away and the room converted for sleeping.

In kitchen and utility areas of the country home, tables tended to be solid and practical. These would be far less elaborate affairs than those found in the living room, for example, where the best pieces of furniture the family could afford would be displayed for the benefit of visitors.

Opposite: *This rustic Adirondack table dates from about 1900.* **Above:** *An early 20th-century marble-topped iron bar table, ideal for a kitchen.* **Below:** *Trestle tables have been popular since medieval times.*

TABLES

The simplest of all manufactured tables was probably made from a rough-hewn cross-section of tree trunk supported on a single column made from a narrower piece of trunk or a broad-based piece of stout root. As tools became more refined and wood-working techniques more sophisticated, however, so the types of table that we are familiar with today began to emerge.

One of the earliest designs of table is the trestle table. This is known to have existed since medieval times and it was still popular

60

BEDS

Bedrooms did not really come into being until late in the Middle Ages, and even then they tended to serve as reception rooms as well as sleeping places. Beds themselves vary

Opposite: *Shaker-style four-posters are perfectly suited to country style.* **Above left:** *Wrought-iron bed ends in a Tuscan bedroom of almost monastic simplicity.* **Above right:** *A Swedish painted pine box bed.*

tremendously in design, from simple wooden platforms with slats of wood to support the mattress to those with elaborately worked brass bed ends holding up a cast-iron bed frame which, in turn, accommodates the mattress. The four-poster has more than a touch of class and elegance to our modern eyes, but it was devised as a practical solution to the problem of sleeping in cold rooms that did not have the benefit of any form of heating. Once inside, with the heavy fabric drapes pulled around, the bed became an intimate, secluded chamber within a chamber, free from the chilling drafts that whistled around just outside. In the hotter states of North America, by way of contrast, beds would be built with an open aspect, elevated from the ground to allow the free circulation of air both around and beneath the bed.

INDEX